This book is primarily a work of fiction. The names, characters, places and incidents are based on the author's imagination. Financial concepts are based on fact and the author's opinion.

First paperback edition 2016

Copyright Number TXu001985102
ISBN 978-0-9977910-3-7 (paperback)

Eleven Digital Group, LLC
New York, NY
info@elevendigitalgroup.com

Visit us at bullbearkidsbooks.com

Adventures in Finance with Bull & Bear

Saving for the Beach

Created By: Roy & Susan Kim

Illustrated By: Surendhra K. Padayatchi

To my wife Susan who worked long and late hours to bring my words to life.

Bull decides he needs a sunny vacation.

He wants to fly on a plane, nap on a beach, and swim in the ocean.

Bull charges to Bear's room to convince her to go. You can tell Bear is thinking, but she just doesn't know.

Then suddenly, "what a great idea", says Bear with a smile.

Bull was happy but shocked. They had not agreed on anything in a while.

Bull and Bear searched for a deal they could afford, and realized they needed money — much more.

Bear shouted, "I told you buying so many games was bad. You should've saved more. Now we're broke... Are you glad?!"

Bull replied, "Don't blame this all on me. What about all your shoes and accessories? Those aren't free!"

This went on forever.
The yelling did not stop.

They were tired and angry and
frustrated and hot.

Eventually they realized that pointing fingers wasn't helping.

They both were to blame for spending and not saving.

The two friends brainstormed ways to raise money. Some were normal and others quite funny.

Bear sold stuff online, and more chores meant longer hours.

Bull dressed up like a princess and sold cookies and flowers.

Bear organized a yard sale on the east side uptown. Bull got a gig on a late night show, dressed up like a panda and jumped around.

Months passed, and they raised enough money for their trip.

They saved exactly the amount they needed plus extra for tips.

They rushed to the computer, and both paused at the door. Bear said, "if we book this trip then our savings will be gone... POOF... no more."

They remembered how hard it was to save. All the work and sacrifices they made every day.

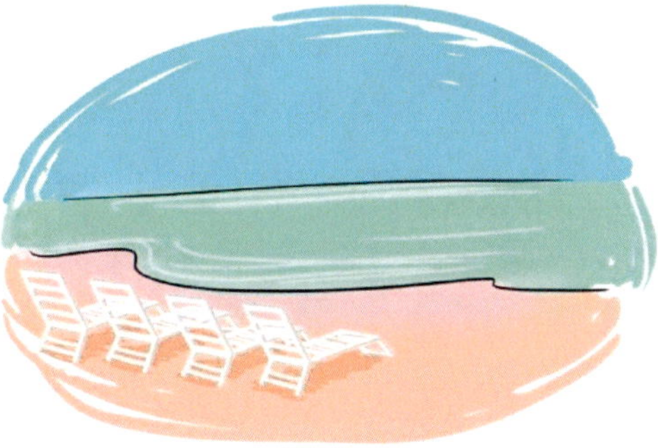

They decided to consider other places to explore. They recalled cheaper choices that still had a shore.

Eventually they made it to the beach. Bull and Bear were happy. Their perfect trip was within reach.

Bear sat in the sun and relaxed in her chair. Bull said, "where to next?" Bear replied, "now that we know we can save — anywhere."

Saving is not very exciting. In fact, it's more like a chore. Bull and Bear learned that when you set aside some money each day, you'll find you can do so much more!

Don't miss the other adventures in our series...

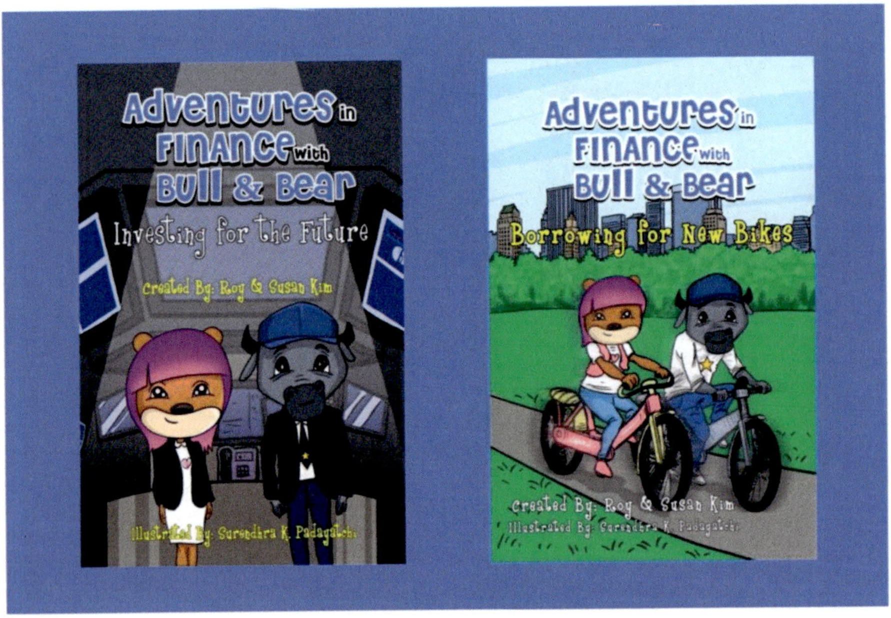

Visit us at BullBearKidsBooks.com

Money Activities

Hey kids! Here are some activities to help you learn more about money and saving. On the next few pages you'll find matching games, word searches, puzzles and more for you to enjoy.

When you finish these activities, ask your parents to help you visit the Bull & Bear Academy at BullBearKidsBooks.com for more **FREE** activities.

MONEY MATCH

Instructions:
First, look at the words and the coins. Draw a line to match a word to the correct coin. Next, look at the coins and the values. Draw a line to match a coin and the correct value.

Words	Coins	Values
Penny		**$0.05** **5¢**
Quarter		**$0.25** **25¢**
Dime		**$0.01** **1¢**
Nickel		**$0.10** **10¢**

COUNTING

Instructions:
Count the coins and draw a line to the correct value.

Coins:

$0.51

$0.31

$1.00

$0.07

$0.52

$0.41

WORD SEARCH

Instructions:
Search for the words in the list below. Circle a word when you find it. Have fun!

List:

Money
Cash
Dollars
Coins
Penny
Nickel
Dime
Quarter
Check
Credit Card
Debit Card
Wire

S	D	E	B	I	T	C	A	R	D	U	M	Q	D
U	P	Z	J	C	G	V	S	V	X	M	V	S	J
H	D	I	M	E	Y	O	C	T	W	P	E	E	K
I	K	P	O	G	P	V	Q	Q	X	C	U	F	Z
X	N	J	N	T	L	E	Q	U	U	R	R	P	M
J	O	T	E	J	M	T	E	A	I	Q	V	E	A
L	T	K	Y	P	R	V	R	R	M	T	O	S	C
Y	O	L	I	S	H	S	T	T	G	G	O	R	Q
S	S	H	K	H	W	B	P	E	O	M	B	A	D
Z	K	E	W	G	M	V	H	R	M	E	D	L	H
W	P	E	N	N	Y	D	C	W	M	R	K	L	X
Q	I	Y	M	I	O	D	O	R	K	I	D	O	I
N	D	B	G	C	Y	H	D	M	C	W	Y	D	E
L	L	G	F	K	H	B	S	O	M	J	A	D	A
L	G	T	M	E	L	E	F	A	U	T	C	Q	Z
X	A	X	Y	L	O	L	C	C	C	Q	I	F	B
X	H	Z	M	W	S	S	J	K	R	O	Z	X	X
G	G	X	X	R	S	T	U	X	K	Y	I	E	J
J	G	R	C	W	H	Z	O	H	M	L	O	N	C
Y	T	K	S	B	I	R	A	T	I	E	T	V	S
S	L	E	K	D	R	A	C	T	I	D	E	R	C

WORD SEARCH

Instructions:

Search for the words in the list below. Circle a word when you find it. Have fun!

List:

Bank	Bitcoin	Balance
Deposit	Currency	Income
Credit	Savings	Teller
Debit	Interest Rate	ATM

I	S	B	A	L	A	N	C	E	P	Q	L	Y	R
T	M	I	G	Y	D	B	Y	X	G	R	H	G	F
X	M	T	F	W	O	V	M	G	S	J	I	T	M
G	Z	C	V	G	Z	H	T	Q	D	G	N	N	B
N	X	O	V	T	U	X	Q	T	V	H	C	A	F
L	B	I	R	X	B	V	Y	H	I	P	O	S	B
K	A	N	Z	T	A	M	C	C	Q	D	M	A	T
R	E	X	B	K	N	P	N	J	R	C	E	S	B
J	E	U	R	D	K	G	E	M	K	Y	C	R	D
J	G	A	K	Y	A	V	R	S	V	H	U	X	C
K	T	M	F	T	C	A	R	G	U	R	R	A	T
M	A	D	S	M	Y	S	U	N	M	E	F	L	O
Y	M	K	C	B	F	R	C	I	Y	L	N	H	M
K	G	Y	D	E	H	U	H	V	F	L	L	M	U
J	U	L	I	P	J	B	U	A	Z	E	X	M	I
B	K	G	N	D	E	P	O	S	I	T	W	M	X
C	P	R	E	V	J	Q	O	V	T	G	E	M	J
J	I	B	C	S	N	C	Q	L	D	Q	O	Q	G
V	I	B	R	T	J	V	P	Y	E	I	F	A	A
T	Y	W	U	B	U	A	M	X	K	T	T	J	S
Q	J	E	T	A	R	T	S	E	R	E	T	N	I

SECRET MESSAGE

Instructions:
Use the decoder below to read the secret message.

Legend:

A	B	C	D	E	F	G	H	I	J	K	L	M
1	2	3	4	5	6	7	8	9	10	11	12	13

N	O	P	Q	R	S	T	U	V	W	X	Y	Z
14	15	16	17	18	19	20	21	22	23	24	25	26

Secret Message:

25	15	21

2	18	15	11	5

20	8	5

3	15	4	5

!

1	19	11

13	15	13

1	14	5

4	1	4

20	15

8	5	12	16

25	15	21

15	16	5	14

1

2	1	14	11

1	3	3	15	21	14	20

1	14	5

19	20	1	18	20

19	1	22	9	14	7

.

SECRET MESSAGE

Instructions:
Use the decoder below to read the secret message.

Legend:

A	B	C	D	E	F	G	H	I	J	K	L	M
1	2	3	4	5	6	7	8	9	10	11	12	13

N	O	P	Q	R	S	T	U	V	W	X	Y	Z
14	15	16	17	18	19	20	21	22	23	24	25	26

Secret Message:

4	15

25	15	21

8	1	22	5

1	14

1	12	12	15	23	1	14	3	5

?

19	5	5

9	6

20	8	5	18	5

1	18	5

3	8	15	18	5	19

25	15	21

3	1	14

4	15

1	20

8	15	13	5

20	15

5	1	18	14

13	15	14	5	25

1	14	4

19	1	22	5

.

HOW MANY WORDS?

Instructions:
Look at the word provided below and see how many different words you can come up with. Write your words in the box provided.

Word:

SAVINGS

Other Words:

HOW MANY WORDS?

Instructions:
Look at the word provided below and see how many different words you can come up with. Write your words in the box provided.

Word:

ALLOWANCE

Other Words:

Made in United States
Orlando, FL
04 November 2026

90203677R00024